Find Your Confidence

by Dr. Katie O'Connell, Ph.D., and Claire Philip

ARCTURUS

For Libby, who shows me what courage looks like.

ARCTURUS

This edition published in 2022 by Arcturus Publishing Limited
26/27 Bickels Yard, 151–153 Bermondsey Street,
London SE1 3HA

Authors: Dr. Katie O'Connell, Ph.D., and Claire Philip
Illustrator: Stef Murphy
Editor: Violet Peto
Designer: Stefan Holliland
Editorial Manager: Joe Harris

ISBN: 978-1-3988-0907-9
CH008351NT
Supplier 29, Date 0821, Print run 10788

Printed in China

Contents

Find Your Confidence!

Everybody feels nervous sometimes—and that's true of even the most confident of people. True confidence isn't about being fearless, but about having the courage to do things even though you feel worried or doubtful. It is a balance between courage and fear.

Finding confidence looks different for everyone because each person's journey has different challenges. As we start on our own unique path, we may come across obstacles. Sometimes overcoming them will feel easy, and other times it may feel hard.

Wow!

The key is to keep trying. Don't focus on the outcome—progress not perfection is your goal! As you learn to face your fears, in time you will realize that they aren't so scary after all. You've got this!

This book gives you the tools to help you find your confidence, with activities and tips for staying cool, calm, and collected when under pressure. Remember that courage begins by taking little steps. As you take small "risks," you build a foundation of confidence. It's a little bit like building a wall, brick by brick.

Who can help you?

You don't have to find your courage alone! We all need a backup team. It can be helpful to write a list of people who are always on your side. Who in your life encourages and supports you? It could be parents, siblings, friends, teachers, or anyone else you can think of. No matter what the outcome, your team will be there to help you get started, pick you up when you fall, and celebrate your successes!

My backup team!

Rate Your Confidence

We each find different situations in life challenging. Belief in your ability, trust in your environment, and your past experiences all shape your confidence when you are called on to be brave.

Rate how confident you feel in each situation by checking the boxes. 1 means "not confident at all." 10 means "very confident."

Eating a new food
Imagine trying a new food when you don't know how it will taste. How would you feel?

1	2	3	4	5	6	7	8	9	10

Learning a new skill
Imagine riding on a skateboard for the very first time. How hard would you find that?

1	2	3	4	5	6	7	8	9	10

Standing out from the crowd
Would you be scared about doing something fun if not all your friends thought it was cool?

1	2	3	4	5	6	7	8	9	10

Trying again

How would you feel about doing something again, if you failed the first time?

| 1 | 2 | 3 | 4 | 5 | 6 | 7 | 8 | 9 | 10 |

Speaking in public

Imagine making a speech at a school assembly—how would you feel? Speaking in front of crowds is a common fear.

| 1 | 2 | 3 | 4 | 5 | 6 | 7 | 8 | 9 | 10 |

Meeting new people

Imagine joining a new club where you don't know anyone yet. Would you find that easy?

| 1 | 2 | 3 | 4 | 5 | 6 | 7 | 8 | 9 | 10 |

Write down a time you have felt brave.

What was the situation? _____

What helped? _____

What would you do differently next time? _____

_____

How it helps

Identifying where you lack confidence is the first step to overcoming your fears. Writing about a time when you have been brave can help you remember the feeling of courage. This can help you apply that feeling again in a different situation.

What Does It Feel Like to Have Courage?

Courage is a choice. It's being ready and willing to face a situation, even though you think there is a risk of some kind. This might be embarrassment, danger, or pain, difficulty, uncertainty, or failure.

If you feel nervous, it simply means that you are stepping outside of your comfort zone. The feeling of courage comes when you try something despite feeling unsure. How you judge your strength, what the risk is, and your ability to manage your fear will all affect your confidence in a situation.

courage   fear

confidence

Fear and courage go hand in hand in any situation that is challenging. Getting the balance right between the two leads to confidence and a positive belief in your own abilities.

Here are some more feeling words associated with courage. Which ones have you felt before? Which ones would you like to feel again?

bold   adventurous

determined

gutsy

strong

patient

daring

8

Here are some examples of children feeling afraid but being courageous anyway. It takes guts to act when you feel fear!

Standing up for yourself is brave.

I don't like scary movies. Can we watch something else?

It's getting high, but I can do it!

How it helps

Knowing that we can feel nervous and courageous at the same time is very important. We can experience fear and still do the thing we want to do. In time, the feeling of fear is replaced with confidence and bravery instead.

It takes courage to keep going!

9

What Is Fear?

Emotions make us act and feel a certain way. Fear might just be the most basic and instinctive emotion because its job is to keep us alive and safe!

When we feel fear, our natural response is to go into a state called "fight, flight, or freeze" to protect our safety. People have felt this response ever since humans first walked the earth. When a prehistoric human was faced with a tiger, they had to make a choice between fighting, running away, or freezing.

Animals in the wild are the same—in a dangerous situation, lions will fight, antelope will run away (flight), and possums will play dead (freeze).

fight   flight   freeze

There are two kinds of fear—real fear and false alarm fear. Real fear is triggered by danger or pain. False alarm fear is the feeling of anxiety or concern about an imagined threat or something that has not happened yet.

The key to building courage is understanding the difference between the two types of fear. If we can slow down our thoughts and recognize false alarm fear, we can continue to build bravery.

If a human doesn't know that everything is okay, an area of the brain called the amygdala is activated. The amygdala controls how you process, react to, and remember emotions.

It receives information (inputs) from all five of your senses and your body systems like your tummy.

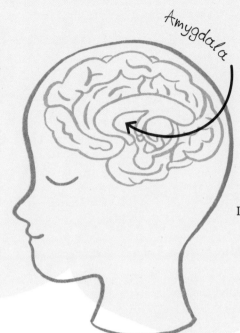

Amygdala

The amygdala sends information (outputs) to your body's alarm system (autonomic nervous system) and does things like change your heart rate, blood pressure, and breathing.

In order to come out of fear, this part of the brain needs to return us to feeling safe.

My body sends me important messages, and I listen to them.

One way to connect to your body and hear its messages is to meditate.

1 Find a comfortable place to sit for five minutes.

2 Sit upright, close your eyes, and take a few deep breaths.

3 As you breathe, notice how your body feels. How does your stomach feel—is it relaxed? How about your jaw? Can you relax all your muscles? See if you can be aware of your whole body at the same time.

4 Focus on your breath—notice how the air fills your lungs as you breathe in and how it feels when it leaves your nose as you exhale.

5 After five minutes has passed, slowly wiggle your toes and fingers and open your eyes.

How it helps

Meditation allows you to quiet the analyzing part of your mind so you can focus on recognizing signals from your body. Over time, meditating will strengthen your balance between feelings and triggering thoughts.

Making Friends with Fear

The next time you notice that you are feeling false alarm fear, remind yourself that you are being challenged by a sense of uncertainty. Start to try being okay with not knowing what comes next. This might feel very difficult at first, but with time, your mind (and body) learns that you are safe.

Is there something right now that you are worried about? Write down two things that could go right and two things that you could learn from the experience no matter what happens.

I'm afraid to go to my new friend's house after school to play.

Two things that could go right:

1 I could have a really nice time!

2 We could play games that I really like.

Two things I could learn no matter what:

1 I could learn social skills.

2 Even if something makes me feel anxious, I am safe—I am not in danger.

Sometimes our fear can signal a need. Maybe we need to feel accepted by our friends, or maybe we need to know that we will be loved, even if we fail. Or maybe we need help and to be shown how to do something a few times.

What do you need from your friends and family? Draw whatever comes to mind in this box.

How it helps

Every single person on Earth has needs. Part of finding your courage is asking for what you need. This is why we have backup teams—these are the people to go to for support.

I'll love you no matter what.

Helping Each Other

It's important to remember that when we start something new, we are beginners—you aren't expected to know everything at once. It can take a long time to learn new skills, so asking for help can be important, especially at the beginning.

We might need help to get something right ..

or be reminded how something is done ..

I can ask for help from others.

or that maybe it's a not a one-person job.

Can you be a helper to someone else?

Ask your teacher if they need help getting the classroom ready.	Ask a parent if they need help with any chores.	Give someone a compliment when you see them trying hard.
Clean up after someone (even though the mess isn't yours!).	Hold the door open for someone.	Bake some cookies for your teacher.
Send thank you cards to your local fire station, police station, or hospital.	If you see someone doing something you know how to do, ask if they would like some help.	If you finish a task first, see if anyone else would like assistance.

How it helps

Giving and receiving help is a two-way street. Helping others lets you put to use the valuable skills you have. Making a positive impact on someone else builds your confidence and self-esteem. You learn that everyone needs and appreciates support from other people.

It's Brave to Talk

Telling someone in your backup team how you feel is an act of bravery. It takes courage to explain your feelings, especially sadness, anger, or fear.

It is important to share our feelings with people we trust. Talking over our feelings makes them more manageable and less overwhelming. Keeping our fear locked up inside gives it no place to go. Once we have shared our worries, we can return to feeling calm and confident. If you are struggling to speak out loud, you could share your feelings in a letter.

Dear Dad,
I have been feeling really worried ...

Use this space here to write down a feeling that you need to share ...

I can ask my teacher to explain something to me ...

I can't remember how to do it. Please will you show me again?

I'm scared.

Me too.

Together!

... or I can ask one of my friends for help.

How it helps

Writing down what you need to say can be very helpful. You get a chance to find the right words, which means that you come across more clearly when you say it in person. Make sure you share your feelings with people you trust, such as your backup team—this will help you feel safe, allowing you to steadily build confidence.

The Confidence to Try

If you want to do something but you also feel like you need to play it safe, you may be thinking about what could go wrong rather than what could go right. The confidence to try is more important than the outcome. You may fall short of your goal, but that is to be expected when you are learning something new.

There are many right ways to do something.

Progress, not perfection, is the name of the game.

I don't have it yet, but I will.

Can you think of some more confidence-boosting statements?

Courage is like a muscle: Each time you take an opportunity to be courageous, you gain strength. This builds confidence over time—even if the outcome isn't exactly what you wanted. Confidence comes when you keep trying and learn what it takes to succeed!

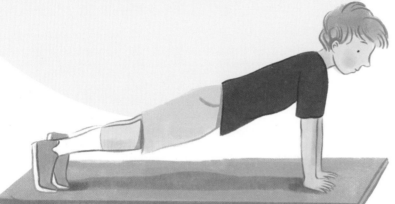

If you have not had the outcome you want, think of a time when you felt your most successful—let yourself remember what that felt like.

Who do you see as confident? Can you list some of their qualities?

_____

_____

_____

_____

_____

_____

How it helps

Asking yourself how a confident person would act in a certain situation can help you act more bravely, as you embody their imaginary actions. There is a well-known phrase, "fake it till you make it," but a better one could be, "fake it till you become it."

Try wearing an outfit that makes you feel great!

What Is Self-Esteem?

Self-esteem is what we think about ourselves. Our relationship with ourselves is the most important relationship in our whole life and is the driving force behind our choices and actions.

Taking on challenges and treating others well creates the basis for good feelings about yourself. Achieving things helps you feel that your life is meaningful. One way to build self-esteem is to experience accomplishments in your life. Your good opinion of yourself grows as you overcome challenges.

I can grow my courage through the choices I make.

Know Yourself. Love Yourself. Be Yourself. Trust Yourself.

I am kind.

Write a list of things you like about yourself in the journal.

I am funny.

I keep trying.

Write down any negative thoughts you may have about yourself below.
Then rephrase your negative thoughts so that they are much more positive!

Negative Thoughts	Positive Thoughts
I am not very confident.	I am learning to find my confidence.
I look different.	I am special and unique!

Having responsibility builds self-esteem. Ask a parent if you can be in charge of feeding the birds. All you need is a bird feeder and some birdseed! Each day, check how many seeds have been eaten, and keep it topped up.

How it helps

How we think about ourselves really matters. By writing down the things that we like about ourselves, we are reminded of how great we are. By writing down our negative thoughts, we give ourselves a chance to challenge these beliefs and rewrite them into something that feels much better. This trains your brain to be kind to yourself. After all, you wouldn't bully another person—so why bully yourself?

Looking After Yourself and Others

Part of being confident is knowing how to look after yourself and others. It takes confidence to speak up and say "NO!" Standing up to a friend or disagreeing with something someone says takes bravery.

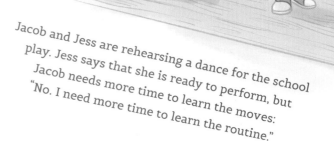

Here are some examples of times it is important to speak up. See how many more you can list.

Jacob and Jess are rehearsing a dance for the school play. Jess says that she is ready to perform, but Jacob needs more time to learn the moves: "No. I need more time to learn the routine."

Hamish is allowed to play in the park as long as he stays inside the playground, but his friend Hayley wants him to leave with her. Hamish has to be brave to say, "No. I am staying here."

Lila can't sleep at her first sleepover. She tells her friend's mother that she would like to go home: "I need to go home. This is what is best for me."

Can you list some more? Have you ever been in a situation like this before? What was it like?

There are also moments that it is appropriate to speak up for someone else.

If you see someone being teased or bullied, report it to a teacher or parent immediately.

If you hear someone talking or joking unkindly about someone else, say, "I don't think that is funny."

If you see someone doing something silly that could be dangerous, tell them, "That's really dangerous, stop!"

Can you list some more? Have you ever had to speak up for someone else? What was it like?

How it helps

Speaking up for yourself and others is an important life skill— it tells the world that you know your values (what is important to you) and that you are determined to uphold and respect them. This is a key part of confidence.

Setting Goals

Now that we have reviewed the many layers of confidence, it's time to set some goals!

Think of two goals that you have been trying to reach or something new that you want to try. Each of your goals will be a focus that accompanies you throughout the rest of the book.

Goal number one

Today's date: _____

My goal is to: _____

_____

What is holding me back? _____

_____

How does that make me feel? _____

Am I safe to try it? _____

What would it feel like to meet my goal? _____

_____

Whether I succeed or not, what could I learn? _____

_____

What do I need to do to start working toward my goal?

_____

_____

Goal number two

Today's date: _____

My goal is to: _____

_____

What is holding me back? _____

_____

How does that make me feel? _____

Am I safe to try it? _____

What would it feel like to meet my goal? _____

_____

Whether I succeed or not, what could I learn? _____

_____

What do I need to do to start working toward my goal?

_____

_____

How it helps

Writing your goals down helps keep them in the forefront of your mind. Examining how you feel about them is important, too, and also asking yourself what could hold you back. This information can help you come up with a plan to tackle obstacles as they arise.

Let's Get Started!

To help you figure out the steps you need to take to work toward each of your goals, try answering some of these questions. Write your answer on the ladder rung next to each question.

My goal is to _____ and this is what I'll do to reach it.

5 How will you know when you've reached your goal?

4 What will you do if you have a setback?

3 What skills do you need to rehearse?

2 Who could you ask for help?

1 What is the first thing you could do to get started?

Write a letter to your future self, congratulating yourself for reaching your goal or working toward reaching your goal. Focus on how amazing it feels, and write about what you learned. Did you have any issues along the way? How did you overcome them?

Dear Future Me,

We did it! I'm so proud of us—I knew we could do it! Even though you felt scared, you kept going and you tried and tried until you got it just right ...

How it helps

Writing a future letter is a great way to move toward your goal because it helps you imagine how it would feel for the goal to be complete. As you write, allow yourself to feel a rush of excitement. This will give you a positive connection to your goal.

Be in the Now

Now that you've figured out your goals and the steps that can help you reach them, you are almost ready to get to work!

Before you start taking action steps, we are going to learn some tools that can help you find calm in moments that may feel challenging. It is completely normal to feel some stress in moments that require bravery.

Three long slow deep breaths ...

The key is to pause and breathe ... to take note of how fear might be affecting you. Very often, we tense up. In the wild, animals have physical ways to release stress through their bodies—they do this through noise or movement. The next time you feel tense about something you need to do, take a seat or lie down and try this muscle relaxation activity.

1 Take three long, slow, deep breaths.
2 Squeeze your feet for three seconds, then relax.
3 Squeeze your legs for three seconds, then relax
4 Squeeze your stomach for three seconds, then relax.
5 Squeeze your upper back and shoulders for three seconds, then relax.
6 Squeeze your arms for three seconds, then relax.
7 Squeeze your whole body for three seconds, then relax.
8 Take three more long, slow, deep breaths.

The next time you feel the tingles of fear, take a moment and try this short activity. You can do it anytime.

Take a long, deep breath. Now ask yourself the following questions:

What can I see?
What can I feel?
What can I hear?
What can I smell?
What can I taste?

How it helps

Learning how to focus on the present moment by paying attention to information from our senses shifts us out of our worried minds and into the present. We stay calm and recognize that we are safe. When we are calm, we can take informed action. If we need to move because there is danger, we can, but if everything is actually okay, we know we are feeling false alarm fear.

Take a Deep Breath

If you are feeling false alarm fear, one of the ways you can soothe yourself is by using your breath. When you breathe deeply, your muscles relax and your blood gets plenty of oxygen. This takes you out of fight, flight, or freeze and into a calm state known as "rest and digest."

Box breathing is a simple exercise to use. Trace the sides of this square with your finger as you breathe in and out to a count of four as shown.

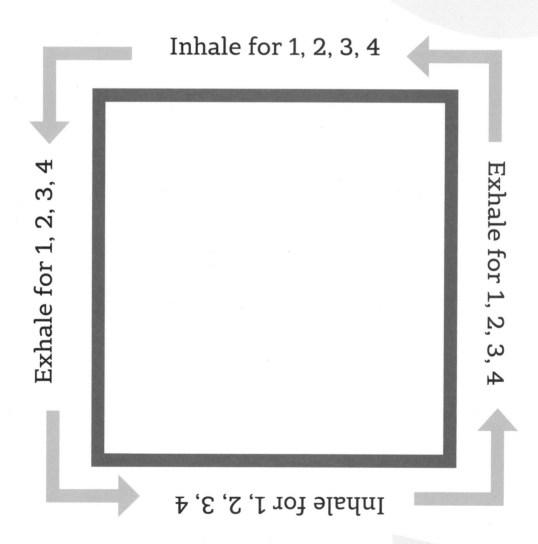

Inhale for 1, 2, 3, 4

Exhale for 1, 2, 3, 4

Exhale for 1, 2, 3, 4

Inhale for 1, 2, 3, 4

Start here

Lion's breath

Lion's breath is great for relieving stress if you feel pent up. Imagine you are a lion, and you have a great big roar to let out! To do it, sit upright and think of a feeling that you would like to let go. Squeeze your hands into tight fists, and scrunch up your face. Take a deep breath in, and then let out your roar. Stick your tongue out, and open up your fists!

Buzz like a bee

Sit comfortably in an upright position and breathe normally. On your next exhale, make the sound "mmmm" with your mouth closed. It should make your lips vibrate. Breathe like this for 30 seconds or so, and see if you feel more relaxed. Top tip: You can cup your hands over your ears to make the noise seem louder!

It's a good idea to work on breath work throughout the day, but you can also set aside some time to do it before you face a challenge.

How it helps

Breath work increases alertness and a sense of clarity so you can have calm focus when tackling challenges. This help us feel more confident.

Worry Box

Have you ever noticed that sometimes a feeling of fear in your body comes after you have been having worried thoughts? While meditating can help us let thoughts pass by, sometimes we need to do something to shift the thought that is making us feel unhappy.

FINISH

Writing your worry down on a piece of paper and placing it in a worry box is a great way to release the thought from your mind. Use a box, such as an empty tissue box, and decorate it with paints.

At bedtime (or any time of the day), write down anything that is bothering you on a strip of paper and put it in the box. Imagine you are handing it over to someone who can take care of it for you. Put the box in a safe place.

A few days later, take out the piece of paper and see if the worried thought has passed. If it has—great! If it hasn't, is there someone on your backup team you could share it with? Make sure to recycle any paper you no longer need.

How it helps

Creating the worry box gives you a safe place to put your worries. Writing down anything that is bothering you helps the feeling know that it has been noticed. Putting it in the box gives you something practical to do to let go of the feeling.

Wash It All Away

Your mind is an amazingly powerful tool. Using your imagination, you can visualize almost anything, including your goals being completed!

Baths and showers are good places to visualize our fears or worries being "washed away." Imagine that the water is soaking you in the feeling of confidence.

worry

anger

sadness

Visualize any fear in your body seeping out into the water and down the drain. Then imagine yourself being bathed in confidence and feeling powerful as you get ready to take action.

bravery

courage

confidence

After you have done your visualization, sit for a few moments and imagine yourself carrying out your goals. You can do this as often as you like!

How it helps

According to scientific experts, visualization tricks the brain into thinking that the images in your mind are real—and it believes it as much as if it was actually taking place. Think how powerful that is! When we visualize something, the brain starts to build a memory of it taking place, which increases your belief that it could happen.

The Power of Laughter

Believe it or not, laughing can help you find your courage! This is because laughter with friends and family—even pets—releases stress. Having a good belly laugh can make your day much better. Laughter connects us with others and takes our focus off whatever is bothering us. It also reduces the stress-related hormones (chemicals) in our bloodstream.

If you feel nervous or fretful, try these activities and have a laugh!

1 Get everyone in your family to pretend to be a puppy or a kitten for five minutes. Who has the most waggly tail?

2 With a friend, see if you can slide a square of chocolate from your forehead to your mouth without using your hands!

3 In a group, choose one person to keep a straight face while everyone else takes turns trying to make them laugh. Who can last the longest?

4 Play musical chairs—sometimes the classics are the best!

5 Dress up. Get out all of your fancy dress clothes (with permission!), and see who can come up with the most hilarious outfit!

How it helps

Laughter has a positive impact on your body. Not only does it give your core muscles a workout, it releases your natural pain-fighting and stress-busting feel-good chemicals (endorphins) to bring you a sense of happiness and peace. Next time you are stressed out, picture yourself having a good laugh and enjoy the soothing buzz that follows!

Ask Your Friends and Family

Sometimes it is helpful to hear other people's stories about how they developed confidence. Ask people in your family to tell you about a time they did something that took courage. Here are some questions you could ask:

1) What was it you feared?

2) What was the risk?

3) How did it feel afterward?

4) What would you have done differently?

5) What did you learn?

After you have spoken to a few people, make some notes on how you can apply what you've learned to your life and your own goals.

Who is your superhero? Pick someone in particular that inspires you with their bravery.
It could be a celebrity, someone you have recently spoken to, maybe a doctor, nurse, firefighter, or police officer. Write down what inspires you about them on the back of the cloak.

How it helps

Talking to people close to you about how they have overcome their own fears can teach you ways of overcoming similar situations in the future. Maybe one day someone will be asking for your advice!

Good Chatter

We have an inner voice that runs a nearly constant commentary on our actions. Listen to what you say to yourself. The more you say something, the more you believe it and make it come true. Are you sending yourself kind messages that will boost your confidence, or are you sending yourself criticism that leads to doubt and fear?

Affirmations are statements that remind us we are capable and confident. By speaking them regularly, we train our brain to feel positive, and when we feel brave and strong, it is much easier to take actions that back that up.

I am brave.

I am confident.

It is safe to be me.

Write out your affirmations on sticky notes, and say them to yourself. Notice how they make you feel.

I love challenges.

I am courageous for trying.

I can reach my goal.

I love learning new skills.

If you try an affirmation and you don't believe that it is true for you, make sure you ask yourself why. Challenge your doubtful thought by asking,
"Is that 100 percent true, all of the time?"
The answer will be "No," of course.

I accept myself whether I win or lose.

I learn from mistakes.

I am safe and loved.

I am important.

I never give up.

Where there is a will, there is a way.

I can do hard things.

How it helps

Our daily thoughts create our realities. When we pay attention to how we speak to ourselves, we may notice an inner critic saying negative things. Affirmations are used to replace these not-so-helpful beliefs.

Healthy Body, Healthy Mind!

Have you ever noticed how much easier it is to be courageous when you feel healthy and relaxed? Studies show that being active is crucial for a healthy body and mind. As we exercise, our bodies produce a chemical called serotonin, also known as the feel-good hormone, which reduces anxiety.

Regular aerobic and strength exercises can also build self-esteem and confidence, as well as connection to others if done in a group setting.

Team sports, running, and games such as tug of war and skipping are other quick and easy ways to get fit and feel good—all of which builds self-confidence.

Eating healthy food and getting quality sleep also keeps our serotonin levels up.

A balanced diet includes plenty of fruit and vegetables, whole grains, and protein such meat, nuts, and seeds.

As we sleep, our sympathetic nervous system, which directs our body's response to stress and danger, takes a break. This means our bodies get a chance to relax and recover.

Six-year-old children need around 10 hours of sleep a night, whereas 12-year-olds need about 9 hours. How many hours do you sleep? Try keeping a sleep diary for a week, and see if you are getting enough shut-eye.

How it helps

Keeping a sleep diary is a great way to monitor how much rest you are getting. This can help you manage stress. Simply make a note of the date, how you slept, the time you went to bed, and the time you woke up. See if you notice any patterns—do you feel braver and more confident when you've had plenty of sleep?

From Fear to Flow

We've learned that fear is a very natural part of being human and that it is important for our survival. Knowing this is helpful, but it doesn't always stop the physical symptoms of fear in the moments before a challenge—especially when we aren't in true danger.

<u>Fear can be experienced</u>
<u>in the body as:</u>

1 Tight muscles
2 Faster heartbeat
3 Quick breathing
4 Fidgeting
5 Clenched jaw
6 Dry mouth
7 Difficultly hearing
8 Shaky hands
9 Flushed skin
10 Fluttering in your belly as digestion slows down

Next time you feel out of your comfort zone, ask yourself: "How am I experiencing fear in my body right now?" Use the list above to help you pinpoint your experience.

Now that you have identified your physical symptoms, try these power poses to help your body move out of fear ahead of a challenging situation. Hold each pose for five breaths, and see if you feel more relaxed and ready to tackle your challenge.

Pose 1

Fingertips reach up toward the sky
Chest is upright and lifted
Front knee is above the ankle
Back leg is straight

Pose 2

Straight arms, stretched out wide
Front knee is above the ankle
Strong legs

I am powerful.

I am focused.

I breathe in risk and uncertainty.

I breathe out courage and confidence.

How it helps

Our posture greatly affects how we feel. Have you ever noticed that if you feel sad or defeated, you round your shoulders forward and lower your head? Our bodies naturally reflect our emotional state. The choice to stand confidently demonstrates your choice to be brave.

Time in Nature

Spending time in nature can help you feel calm and safe. This is because what we hear, see, and experience at any moment affects our bodies—specifically our blood pressure, muscle tension, and even our immune system. When our surroundings are peaceful, our bodies can feel peaceful, too!

Ask an adult to take you on a walk. You could visit a park, some woodland—even the beach! As you go, see if you can spot a special stone, pine cone, or shell that will fit in your pocket.

Play with your item in your pocket if you feel nervous before a challenge. As you do so, remember how peaceful you felt in the outdoors. Let these memories of nature soothe you—then go for it!

Earthing, also known as grounding, is another outdoor activity that can reduce fear and bring you closer to confidence.

The next time you are on a nature walk, take off your shoes and socks and try this pose to connect to the ground.

1 Stand up tall, with your feet close together.

2 Allow your body to settle—don't worry if you sway a little bit at first.

3 Try to balance your weight evenly between your feet.

4 Focus on your posture—push your shoulders back and down.

5 Let your arms hang loosely by your sides.

6 Breathe deeply, and hold the pose for five to ten breaths, feeling your connection to the ground and how supported you are.

How it helps

Even though it looks easy, it is actually quite difficult to stand in proper alignment for more than a few minutes! Holding this simple posture is a great way to slowly yet powerfully build strength and stability.

Dance and Stomp

Feeling a little bit anxious? Get up, stomp your feet, and dance! Dancing is an amazingly uplifting activity that gives you lots of energy. It also helps tension leave the body, which dramatically reduces fear—it's hard to feel nervous when you are moving your entire body!

Put the radio on, or play a song.

Let loose to the music, and dance like no one is watching!

Move as much as you can. Don't hold back!

Feel free to clap and sing loudly as you go!

You could also try dance classes such as ballet, jazz, salsa, or hip-hop. Dance classes build comfort and security in being in your body. As you rehearse and master routines, you build confidence in your strength, coordination, memory, and reflexes. Dancing works out your body and your mind!

How it helps

Humans are not supposed to be stationary all the time! We are meant to move and flow. Dancing is a very freeing exercise that takes you out of your head and into your body, especially if you've spent lots of time sitting down. Try it if you are feeling stressed out by homework.

Powerful Poetry

Writing poetry is an incredible way to capture feelings in just a few words. Learning how to write poems will help you discover a powerful way to express yourself and deal with uncomfortable feelings, such as fear. The power of imagination makes you limitless!

Before you start writing poetry, it might be useful to read or listen to some poems by other people and see which ones stand out to you. You can look in books or research online.

When I think of the space
under my bed,

I feel a growing sense
of dread ...

I turn on my light

And no longer feel fright

There is nothing there,

No monsters to scare!

Is there a feeling that you would like to express right now? Here are some tips for writing poetry that makes you feel empowered:

- Make time to write away from doing homework.

- Choose a quiet space to write.

- Don't worry about how "good" any of your writing is.

- Use repetitive phrases. For example, you could start and finish each line of a poem about courage with: "And still I try."

- Use comparisons, such as "as brave as a lion."

- Use funny or nonsense words, such as "I am fantabulous!"

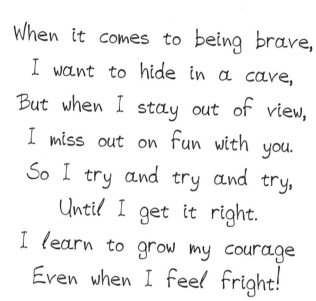

When it comes to being brave,
I want to hide in a cave,
But when I stay out of view,
I miss out on fun with you.
So I try and try and try,
Until I get it right.
I learn to grow my courage
Even when I feel fright!

How it helps

Writing about a feeling or experience gives you some control over it. You can safely and privately explore it, shape the images and story the way you want, and edit it if and when you please. Acknowledging your feelings in writing is an act of bravery.

Draw Your Feelings

Drawing is a visual language that lets you disconnect from the whir of chatter and technology. Not only does it relieve stress, but it also aids relaxation, much like meditation. Sketching is a physical act that lets you express your ideas, observations, and feelings in a creative way and gives your mind a break from problem-solving and focusing. Try these art activities, and see if they make you feel calm. Make a note of how you feel before and after.

Before:

1	2	3	4	5	6	7	8	9	10

After:

1	2	3	4	5	6	7	8	9	10

1 means, "I feel stressed and worried," while 10 means "I feel calm and competent."

In the heart shape, draw whatever is in your heart right now using pencils or crayons. You may wish to draw shapes, swirls, and spirals, or you may want to draw pictures of people, animals, or places.

What does fear look like?

For this exercise, use pencils or crayons to show how fear would look if it had a physical form. Would it be dark purple like a storm cloud or bright yellow like lightning?

How it helps

Sketching and doodling have been shown to trigger the body's relaxation response. Drawing helps pause worried thinking because it soothes the mind into integrating the fingers, hand, and arm, with its thinking, emotional, and motor systems.

Make a Comic Book

Use this comic book template to draw yourself performing one of your goals. Plan what could be in each box before you start, and draw in pencil first. Once you are happy with your design, use crayons to finish it. In the last box, show yourself celebrating! Top tip: Draw yourself standing in a superhero pose to show off your confidence!

Get Musical!

Making music works out nearly all parts of your brain and sensory systems. As you learn to sing or play an instrument, you build your confidence in working hard to learn new skills and reaching goals. You can also increase your creativity and planning skills through improvisation.

recorder

If you play music or sing in a group, it can also help you form friendships. A sense of belonging is important for confidence, too—the more people in your backup team, the better!

Which instrument would you like to try?

violin

saxophone

Try making a power playlist of all the tunes that make you want to get up, dance, and sing! You could listen to it as you draw or play, as well as before you start working at reaching your goals.

drum

keyboard

Make your own musical instrument! This quick and easy activity takes very little time and is a great place to start if you don't already play an instrument.

guitar

1 First, you will need a clean tin can. Ask an adult to make sure that the can has no sharp edges. Fill the can with rice.

2 Stretch an empty balloon over the top.

3 Secure it in place with a rubber band.

You can shake it so that it rattles, or you can use a pencil to tap the top of the drum!

Performing music in front of people is a common fear. Try playing your new instrument at home in front of your family to shake off those performance nerves!

How it helps

Making music lets you manage your nervousness while acting in real time. You can start over, correct mistakes immediately, or keep going despite errors. Then you can try again with feedback. Musical performance is active learning! You not only get a second chance, but many chances to improve different qualities like speed, tone, emotional expression, and dramatic pausing.

Get Moving!

Let's focus on large muscle movement now. Knowing where your body is in space is critical to feeling strong and courageous. You build agile body awareness and strength by doing all kinds of outside activities. Try some of these examples to get your game on, and just see how your coordination and confidence grow!

Go on a hike to improve your core, spine, leg strength, and balance.

Running strengthens your legs, lungs, and heart.

Learn to skate and improve your balance.

Soccer improves acceleration, leg strength, pivoting, speed, and agility.

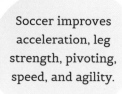

Cycling improves visual scanning, It also strengthens your quad muscles and balance.

Playing basketball builds teamwork, strategy skills, full body coordination, and body control.

Swimming tests your aerobic and anaerobic endurance.

Ice skating improves balance and flexibility.

Bowling improves hand-eye coordination.

Archery improves your concentration.

Riding a horse gives you strong core muscles.

Climbing helps you build strength—especially in your upper body.

How it helps

Experts agree that regular physical activity builds self-esteem, feelings of empowerment, and optimism. Being strong and fit make you more resilient to stress.

Plan for Success

A little anxiety is a good thing when it comes to taking tests because it motivates you to prepare and focus. However, too much anxiety can distract you from your task. Being well prepared puts your mind at ease and keeps anxiety from escalating out of control. Research shows that cramming increases anxiety and undermines your best efforts.

Test-taking strategies

1 Prepare—learn all you can about the material and the test ahead of time, so there are no last-minute surprises.

2 Listen to your inner voice—be careful about what you are telling yourself and try to be self-encouraging.

3 Visualize success—picture yourself feeling confident and clearheaded during your test.

4 Use relaxation strategies, such as deep breathing, to ease feelings of tension and fear.

5 Arrive early—rushing increases anxiety. When you get there, you will have time to prepare your mind.

6 Focus—if you get distracted or mixed up, have some strategies to mentally regroup—put your pencil down and take a deep breath. Then start up again refocused and calm.

7 Give yourself time at the end to read through your answers and, make sure you've answered every question.

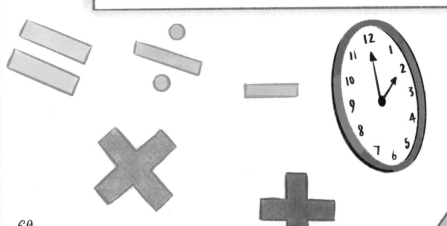

You can also develop your strategy skills by playing games such as chess or charades. Chess helps you develop logical thinking, and charades builds your non-verbal communication skills. Both teach you valuable skills that add to self-confidence.

How it helps

Everyday situations call for us to be strategic. For example, when we meet new people, we think of ways to approach them and make a good impression. At school, we follow learning strategies. Having strategies allows us to think ahead, giving ourselves time to feel prepared when facing challenging situations. This builds confidence and self-belief.

Trying New Foods

Replace your food fear with curiosity! Remember that you have choices and control over what you eat. Trying new foods can be fun.

If you are someone who really doesn't like trying new foods and you would like to get better at it, try answering the following questions:

1 What is blocking you from trying new food?

2 What is the worst thing that could happen?

3 Would you be okay if that happened?

4 What is the best thing that could happen?

5 What steps would help you get to that outcome?

Vegetables are good for us but can take a little getting used to.
Try making your own delicious carrot brownies to get the carrots' nutrients without the strong taste.

Ingredients

200 g (7 oz) baking chocolate · 100 g (½ cup) butter · 3 eggs
200 g (1½ cup) sugar · 1 tsp vanilla extract · 100 g (¾ cup) self-rising flour
25 g (3 tbsp) cocoa powder · 200 g (1½ cup) carrots, grated (ask an adult to help you)

Method

1) Preheat the oven to 180°C (350°F)

2) Line a 20 cm (8 in) square pan with parchment paper.

3) Ask an adult to help you melt the chocolate and butter in a mixing bowl over a pan of simmering water.

4) Remove from the heat, and add the eggs, sugar, and vanilla to the batter. Stir until smooth.

5) Add the flour, cocoa powder, and carrots. Stir all the ingredients together until well mixed.

6) Pour the batter into the pan, and bake for 30 minutes until it is springy to the touch.

7) Leave to cool, then sprinkle with some powdered sugar and slice into squares.

How it helps

Trying a new recipe is an amazing way to bring enjoyment to eating. As you combine the ingredients, maybe even getting your hands messy, you become far more connected to what you eat and gain a sense of pride as you dish up your meal.

Survival Skills

Courage is built over time and in lots of different situations. One great way to develop a sense of confidence and independence is to learn survival skills, such as map-reading and navigation. Like other learned skills, they broaden your knowledge, which allows you to do more and gives you the feeling that you can take on more challenges.

Learning how to understand map symbols and how to navigate across a landscape opens up a world of adventure to you!

Planning a camping trip is great for gaining confidence as it builds self-responsibility and preparedness. Write a list of everything you would need for a night under the stars, and go camping with a parent or trusted adult. Did you remember everything you needed?

How it helps

Planning for an expedition (even a short trip) helps you learn that you are fully capable of preparing for a new situation, which builds confidence and self-trust.

Unleash Your Inner Artist

Paint, glue, cut! Arts and crafts are great fun. They are also excellent confidence builders—as you explore your creativity and make things, you feel a sense of accomplishment.

Crafts allow for self-expression, which is incredibly important for happiness and self-esteem. It encourages thinking, exploring, imagining, and discovering, all at once!

The famous artist Henri Matisse once stated that "creativity takes courage." He believed that sharing art with others is a vulnerable act of bravery. As you share something you've painted or made that is personal to you, you take the risk of being judged by others. You can do it!

Rock painting

1 Gather some oval pebbles on a walk, and wash them off.
2 Plan your design, and draw it on the rock in pencil first.
3 Use acrylic paints to bring your designs to life.
4 Once the paint has dried, use varnish or PVA (craft) glue to seal the paint and make it weatherproof.

Lots of crafts involve constructing—for example, you could make a cardboard castle or even a puppet. These kinds of activities involve problem-solving skills, which when mastered, build self-esteem and confidence. Others involve figuring out patterns, such as beading, mosaics, and weaving. These kinds of creative projects encourage mindfulness, too.

How it helps

When you regularly express yourself through art, you build a strong sense of who you are—and you learn that you are highly capable of whatever you set your mind to. This is a huge building block of confidence—you are a powerful creator! Crafts also help connect people and build a backup team!

Making Friends

No matter how old you are, it can take a little bit of time to make new friends—and it always takes courage. Try this role play activity with someone in your backup team to rehearse making introductions.

Step 1
Get together with a parent or someone in your backup team, and talk about making friends. Discuss how you feel and your worries before you start your role play.

Step 2
Add as much detail as you can. Where are you? Are you in a classroom, or maybe on the school bus? Who else is around, and what is everyone else doing?

Step 3
Take turns playing the person asking to be friends and the person being asked.

"Please may I sit next to you?"

"Yes, sure."

"Do you have any pets?"

Step 4
Act out the scenario the best you can. What follow-up questions can you think of to keep the conversation going?

Here are some tips to help you on your way.

Ask them a question, for example, "What's your name?" or "Would you like to sit with me at lunchtime?"

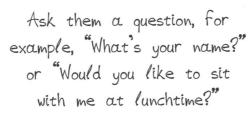

When you meet someone new, say hello to show the other person that you are friendly, and make sure to smile.

Share your toys or ask them if they might like to play a game or do something together.

Ask questions! People love to talk about the things they like and their hobbies.

Remember to be kind and thoughtful—whether you are talking to someone else or they are talking to you.

How it helps

Courage multiplies what you are today into what you might become in the future, so the more you work on friendship today, the easier it will be in the future! Learning how to relate to others is incredibly important. Some people will have different ideas and opinions to you—and that is okay. Throughout your life, you will meet many people with different beliefs and priorities. Being able to see that everyone has their own reality helps you connect with them, and feel confident.

Joining Clubs

If you are thinking about, or are currently joining a new club, you may worry about how you might fit in. That's a totally normal feeling! Joining clubs can be daunting for everyone, but they can push you to discover different parts of yourself, help you develop friendships, and form lasting bonds with other people.

Clubs help you use up extra energy! Do you feel like you need to move around or do something when you get home from school? A club can give you something to focus on and enjoy.

These group activities help you make friends. Widening your friendship circle is a very positive thing that comes from clubs. You get to try out meeting new people and forming bonds. You may also meet a wider variety of people, which makes life more interesting.

Clubs can be great for exercise. During school hours, there isn't always much time to move about and exercise, but clubs such as dance, gymnastics, or karate, for example, provide plenty of opportunity to build confidence by becoming more physically confident. Move around, and get those happy, feel-good hormones pumping!

Taking part in shows, games, and matches gives you a sense of achievement. As you progress, you see that you can do whatever you set your mind to. Some clubs will give badges and awards to reward hard work. It feels great to be told congratulations!

How it helps

Joining a club or group is a great way to feel a sense of belonging. A club can challenge your emotional and physical limits and push you to grow. Once you've settled in and made some new friends, you will have another place that you feel safe—which is a building block for confidence.

Saying No

Saying "No" to something that doesn't feel right is one of the bravest things a person can do. If someone asks you to do something you don't want to do or you do not feel comfortable doing, it is okay to say no.

What is peer pressure?

Peer pressure is the term used for social situations that make you feel as though you have to do something in order to fit in with the crowd. These situations can require you to be brave and stand up for yourself by saying no.

Saying no is powerful

- Saying no keeps you safe and tells other people if something is not okay with you.

- Saying no helps you know who you are. You are in charge of the actions you take, the things you like, and your own opinions.

- Saying no builds confidence. When you can stand up for yourself, you develop strength and independence.

- Saying no to doing something is not the same as rejecting a person. It is important to learn that it is normal for people to disagree.

- Saying no can be easier to start with if you explain why not.

Saying "No" is brave.

Deciding not to do something is the first step. The tricky part—finding a way out—is the next step and not only requires bravery but careful thinking. Having a plan ahead of time will boost your resolve. Here are some options to try:

A firm but polite no

> No, I don't want to, thanks.

Leaving or walking away

> No, thank you, I don't want to. See you tomorrow at school.

Suggesting an alternative— something else to do instead

> "No, thank you, I don't feel like doing that. How about building a fort?"

Explain the rules your parents or teachers have set

> No, I can't come over—my dad says I have to go home to do my homework.

How it helps

Learning how and when to say no is something that lots of people (even adults) find difficult. Getting to grips with it as a child is a powerful thing. It helps you put your needs first, which helps you say YES to what matters the most to YOU. Successful people are comfortable saying no as it allows them to focus on their goals with confidence and without distraction.

Learn to Stop Bullying

Bullying is wrong because it hurts, intimidates, or excludes another person. The bully should be called out and stopped. This takes courage.

A bully is someone who ...

- picks on others using words or physical strength
- steals or damages someone's belongings
- excludes someone from a group
- makes threats
- uses technology such as social media to send unkind messages
- spreads gossip about someone

What does bullying look like?

Sometimes bullies use words to hurt or embarrass someone. Other times they use physical strength to hit or push someone. The result is always the same—someone becomes sad and feels uncertain about their place in the group.

No one deserves to be bullied.

What to do if you are being bullied

Try to calmly yet firmly say "NO, LEAVE ME ALONE" or "STOP IT." Walk away to a crowded place or toward other friends or adults. Then, speak to an adult you trust—someone from your backup team or a teacher.

Bullying is never the target's (victim's) fault.

What to do if you see someone else being bullied

If you see someone being bullied or deliberately left out of a group, do not smile or laugh. Bullies look for a reaction. If you can, tell the bully that they need to stop what they are doing, but only if it is safe to do so. It is important to show that you disagree with the actions of the bully, but you must take care of yourself, too. Always tell a teacher or an adult what is happening.

Remember that you don't have to deal with this alone—you have a backup group to go to. If you would like to speak to someone you don't know about it, there are helplines that you can call at the end of this book.

How it helps

Saying no to bullying is powerful. Knowing that you can stand up bravely and say "No" to unkind actions is a sign of true courage.

Speak up for the Planet

Our planet needs lots of care and attention—and it needs confident people like you to stand up and say that we must do more to take care of the environment. Making change starts with small, everyday actions. You and your family's habits will have a big impact on your world over time.

You can begin now to courageously change our planet for the better by recycling, reusing, and reducing. Here are some ideas.

Donate toys and sports equipment you no longer use to a charity

Ask your parent to buy you a reusable water bottle.

Recycle your cans, bottles, glass, and paper.

Speaking up for issues that you think are important takes courage. Discuss your ideas with your backup team and your friends.

How it helps

Speaking up for an important cause helps build confidence throughout your life—not just as a kid. By taking care of nature as a child, you pave the way for a life of care and consideration for the planet—you learn that your choices have consequences and that small actions have huge effects.

Journal Your Way to Confidence!

Writing a journal is an inexpensive strategic tool right at your fingertips. All you need is a pencil and paper to get started.

A journal gives you a place to record your inner voice! You can put down your thoughts and feelings. Through writing, you can listen to your thoughts without judgement, fear, or ridicule. You will have time to work on solitary reflection and self-love.

Try these journal prompts:

• How have you shown courage recently?

_____

_____

• What are your three greatest strengths?

_____

_____

Write about someone who inspires you.

What is it about them that inspires you?

Write about a time when you used strategies
to overcome a challenge.

How did it feel?

How it helps

The process of writing increases your skill level, stamina,
and desire to persevere, and it helps you to not give up. It gives
you space to refine your goals, recommit to your actions, find
creative solutions, and try out "What if" contingency plans.

I Belong

Every single person on the planet needs to feel a sense of belonging. It helps us to feel safe and supported. When we know that we belong to a family, a friendship group, a club, or a community, we feel more confident. This is because it is easier to take risks when we know we have a place in the world and that we are understood.

Here are some things you can do to strengthen the bonds with your family. The more united we feel, the more courage we can muster!

1 Create a new family dance—the more bizarre, the better!

2 Hold a movie night every two weeks, and take turns choosing what you watch.

3 Make time for a story with a family member each night before bed.

4 Go on a full moon walk. There's a full moon roughly every month. Take a short walk at night as a family to look at it.

In friendship groups, a sense of belonging can be encouraged by celebrating each other's good points. Gather your friends together, and take turns complementing each person, one at a time. Remember, it is okay if you or someone else wants to pass.

accepted

Timmy is really funny.

listened to

Timmy is very kind.

loved

valued

Building a sense of belonging is also about being inclusive—thinking of those who may feel left out. It is not about being in a special group that others can't join.

liked

missed if I'm absent

What does it mean to you to belong?

_____

_____

Where are some of the places you belong?

_____

_____

How it helps

Knowing where you belong helps you recognize the feeling of being accepted for who you are. This helps you express yourself freely and confidently since you know you are safe and cared for.

Being Grateful

Studies show that being thankful for the good things that come your way increases your confidence and gives you the courage to face new challenges. Don't dwell on negative thoughts, and instead think of all of the wonderful things in your life. When you feel good, you are more likely to put yourself out there, meaning you reap the rewards of confidence.

"I am grateful for my cat."

How to be grateful

Step one: Think of someone, something, or somewhere that you feel thankful for. Has someone been kind to you recently, done something for you, or given you a gift?

Step two: Think about why it feels good to be treated kindly and generously.

Step three: Write a list of the feelings this brings up.

Step four: Do something to show the person you are thankful for their kindness.

happy

excited

lucky

proud

loved

Start a gratitude jar

Each time you notice someone that makes you grateful, write it down on a piece of paper and place it in a "gratitude jar." Every couple of months, take them all out and read them.

How it helps

Gratitude is a mindset that can become a habit if we train our brain to think positively. As we grow up, we experience emotional bumps and grazes. It is easy to hold on to the unpleasant sensations that arise from them, but if we direct our attention to the good things in life, the negatives will fade into the background. Learning to tap into positive feelings is a seriously powerful skill that allows you to access happiness whenever you like!

Reflect on Your Bravery Journey

Now that you have been working on your courage and met parts of your goals, take stock of your growth so far.

Consulting with yourself is key to keeping your confidence increasing. You've hopefully started to make friends with your mind and learned how to turn the volume down on your inner critic as you've tried some new things.

Use this space to reflect on your bravery journey so far.	How have you grown in your awareness of where you feel challenged?
How have your beliefs about your confidence and ability to cope grown?	How have you connected to friends and your backup team in a new way?

I am growing and improving.

This means I will learn from others.

Mistakes help me learn.

This may take time, but I'll get there.

Feedback from others helps me learn.

I like learning new things.

Look at the bricks in the bravery wall. What are the attributes and feelings you are still working on?

How it helps

Self-reflection helps build self-esteem, which will make your next challenge a little easier as you grow in confidence. This time, you won't be starting from scratch—you'll be able to refer back to the lessons you learned. A key to self-reliance, self-reflection helps you alter your course and stay on the path to your goals.

For Parents

Explain confidence and lead by example

Challenging events and uncertainty inevitably occur in our children's lives. Some kids will choose challenging goals (e.g., like trying out for a sports team) or experience difficult life events (e.g., divorce, sickness). While we can't control what challenges our kids will face, we can help set them up to meet them head on. Our kids need to feel confident enough to deal with difficult situations and to try new things nearly every day. It is our job as parents to guide them along their way.

As parents, we help our kids to gain perspective and problem-solve. We show them how to not overreact to failure or not minimize their successes.

Perhaps the most important lessons you can teach your kids is that challenges are a normal part of life faced by everyone—and that no one is perfect or expected to be perfect, especially when learning or trying something new.

Research shows that kids who think it is okay and normal to fail many times when trying something new, persist at problem-solving. On the other hand, kids who believe that failure is humiliating and a sign that they are incompetent, are less inclined to persevere with problem-solving.

Kids need to understand that challenges are opportunities for learning and getting stronger. When kids have this perspective, they will worry less and focus more on increasing their skill and learning.

Kids also need to learn to cope with intense feelings such as anger, sadness, disappointment, jealousy, and frustration that often accompany trying new things or overcoming challenges. To do this, they need to notice their feelings, label the emotion, then make a connection between the feeling and the situation that triggered it.

Talking with your kids about their feelings and helping them find words to express themselves is one of the best ways to start. Have a conversation about confidence and what it means, and listen to how they currently feel about themselves. You can explain that confidence comes when we know that we will be fine, even when experiencing difficult emotions. It comes from self-belief and a feeling of being sure of your abilities.

Kids need to know that confidence levels change depending on how we feel and in each individual situation. We won't build confidence, however, if we don't try new things and get outside of our comfort zone. So setting an example to your child by consciously working on your own self-confidence can be an enormous help. Be aware of the language you use around your kids—if they hear you referring to yourself negatively, they may start to believe the same of themselves.

How do you know when your child is struggling with confidence?

You may notice that your child finds small changes very challenging or that they are increasingly worried about fitting in with friends. Other signs are being reluctant to try new things or becoming overly concerned about failing. Sometimes kids may have wildly changing moods or intense emotions that seem to come from nowhere.

For Parents

Let them know they are not alone

Regularly tell your child that they have a backup team. Family
relationships are so important for our health and well-being—when
a child feels secure in their belonging, they will be more confident
in the outside world. Tell them who is in your backup team, too.

Focus on solutions rather than problems

Helping a child come up with a step-
by-step plan to reach their goal can be
priceless. If they can see that there are
lots of stages to take rather than one
giant leap, they may be more willing to
slowly ease in to building their brave.

Ask how they want to be supported

It can be very easy to push a child into building their confidence before they are ready. We must remember that childhood can be an overwhelming time—kids are finding out who they are in relation to their body, their family, friends, peers at school, and the wider community, including online.

Taking small steps is key—as well as prioritizing listening to their feelings and not taking what they say personally. If a child absolutely refuses to do try something, we have to respect that—after all, we want them to be able to stand up for themselves as adults.

Often, more can be gained by deep listening to our children and helping them feel safe rather than edging them toward activities that they might not be ready for—even if we can see the enormous benefits for them. Don't give up, but actively stay calm and open to them coming forward in their own time. Keep giving opportunities, but let them know that when they are ready, you will be there to help them, no matter what feelings it brings up for them.

"How can I support you?"

For Parents

Explain how you deal with fear

Try talking to your children about how you have dealt with fear in the past—and how you do so now. Make sure you give examples of relatable challenges that you have overcome, and let them know that you can relate to feelings of nervousness or resistance. In essence, offer them empathy.

Make affirmation notes

A great activity to do together is to choose confidence affirmations. Stick them somewhere in the house for everyone to see. You can either keep them up for a long time or change them regularly, depending on whatever challenges your kids are going through.

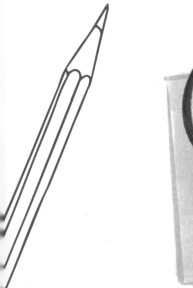

I can do this.

I am grateful for every day.

Praise improvements and give genuine compliments

Your attention and messages have a powerful impact on your child's self-confidence. Be mindful of where your focus lies. Are you paying attention to and praising the results of your child's efforts (e.g., scoring a goal or getting an A) more than on their effort itself? Kids develop by successive approximation, which means that with each attempt they get closer and closer to the desired outcome. Paying attention to their efforts helps them to stay positive while taking on challenges. It is easy for kids to give up and throw in the towel when the final outcome is in the future and seems out of reach. Saying things like, "I really admire how you stuck with it, even though you were frustrated," or "Wow, you worked so hard in the game. Which part are you most proud of?" are ways of shifting the focus from achievement and onto your child's process of developing. Send the message that you are watching and cheering for their hard work, and you are noticing their improvement. By asking them questions about their efforts, you give them the chance to reflect on their skills, strategies, and obstacles. Having these conversations builds their confidence for next time. When they do bring home that A or score the winning goal, be sure to give them a hug and high five, but also give them a chance to tell you about the process and how their persistence helped them reach their goal.

For Parents

Remember that children replicate what they can see

It sounds simple, but ensuring that you take care of yourself well is powerful. Having a healthy lifestyle, eating well, sleeping consistently, and prioritizing learning and exercise in your own life can inspire children to do the same. They are more likely to learn by example than being told how to behave.

As you go through life making choices, some of which may involve facing fears of your own, if appropriate, talk about your decision-making process with them. Let them know how you decide whether or not to do something, and explain how you manage risk in your own life.

This can help teach children to plan before they take action and also see that their actions can influence outcomes. If you demonstrate trust in life, they will, too.

Give children small, age-appropriate responsibility

Put clothes in laundry basket	✓
Help put away bowls and plates after dinner	✓
Feed pets	
Help put food shopping away	✓
Tidy room	
Help clean out the car	

Glossary

Aerobic exercise
A kind of exercise that encourages oxygen through the blood and often makes you breathe more deeply, for example, running or cycling.

Anaerobic exercise
A kind of exercise tht is high intensity, fast, and that can only be maintained for short bursts. For example, sprinting or rowing.

Affirmations
Words or phrases that you say about yourself, also called self-talk.

Amygdala
The small part of the human brain that coordinates our emotional responses to things.

Anxiety
A feeling of worry or dread about something that has not happened yet—future-oriented worry.

Bravery
The experience of feeing afraid but believing that you can overcome it.

Confidence
The belief that you can rely on yourself, someone else, or something.

Coordination
The ability to use the body and its senses to perform certain tasks accurately, such as throwing a ball at a target.

Cortisol
Often called the "stress hormone," our bodies produce this chemical when we feel high levels of stress, This hormone also manages our blood sugar levels.

Creativity
New ways of thinking, problem-solving, or making something using imagination.

Earthing
The ancient practice of walking or playing barefoot outdoors to experience the health benefits of nature.

Emotions
Feelings that we experience. They can be influenced by our surroundings, moods, and relationships, meaning they are changeable.

Hormones
The chemicals produced by the body that affect many different physical processes, such as growth and development. They travel in your bloodstream.

Intuition
The ability to understand or know something without using logical reasoning.

Meditation
A practice involving mindfully noticing whatever is happening right now, without becoming attached to it.

Reflexes
Movements that the body makes without making a decision to do so, for example, moving your hand away from something hot before it burns.

Self-esteem
High self-esteem is when you have great confidence in your worth and value; low self-esteem is when you doubt these things.

Serotonin
A hormone produced by the body that is thought to regulate our moods, including happiness and anxiety.

Subconscious
The part of the mind of which we are unaware. It stores our memories and skills.

Sympathetic nervous system
This body system is also known as the fight or flight response, when the body is under threat or in danger.

Visualization
The use of your imagination to create a mental image of a desired outcome.

Vulnerability
The state of being exposed to others or situations that are possibly harmful.

Further reading

There are lots of storybooks out there that feature brave characters. See which ones inspire you the most!

Shy by Deborah Freedman

Tomorrow I'll be Brave by Jessica Hische

Bold & Brave by Kirsten Gillibrand, illustrated by Maira Kalman

Little Tree by Loren Long

If you need more help

If there is ever a time that you want to speak to someone that you don't know about a problem, you can contact these organizations. The people that work there are specially trained to help children with any kind of problem—you can tell them absolutely anything. It's important to remember that there is always something that can be done to make a situation better, no matter what.

North America

kidshealth.org
With sections for parents, kids, and teens, this is what most pediatricians use for education.

girlshealth.gov
A website specifically for girls, this has lots of great information about feelings, relationships, and biology.

healthfinder.gov
Mostly for parents, this has lots of good advice articles.

adaa.org
The specific website of the Anxiety and Depression Association of America.

worrywisekids.org
Accessible to both kids and adults, this is a great source of information on anxiety and depression.

UK

Childline
Help and advice about a huge range of issues. Comforts, advises, and protects children 24 hours a day, and offers free, confidential guidance by helpline, online chat, and Ask Sam. childline.org.uk or call 0800 1111

The Samaritans
Listening and support for anyone who needs it. Contact 24 hours a day, 365 days a year—calls and emails are free and confidential. samaritans.org or call 116 123

NHS
healthforkids.co.uk/feelings/
You can always talk to your family GP about your feelings.

Australia & New Zealand

Kids Helpline (telephone and online guidance for ages 5–25)
kidshelpline.com.au or call 1800 55 1800

Youthline
youthline.co.nz
Free call 0800 376 633
Free text 234

Index

A
achievements 20, 71
affirmations 18, 40–1, 90–1
amygdala 11
anxiety 10, 42, 60
art 52–5, 66–7

B
backup teams 5, 13, 16–17, 33, 56, 68, 75, 77, 88–9
baths/showers 34–5
belonging, sense of 56, 71, 80–1
brain 11, 35, 40, 56, 83
bravery 7–10, 16–17, 19, 43, 45, 51, 66, 72–3, 84–5, 88
breathing exercises 11, 30–1
bullying 23, 74–5

C
calmness 28–30, 60
caring 22–3, 75
challenges 20, 31, 44–6, 82, 86, 90–1
clubs 70–1
comfort zones 8, 44, 87
comic books, making 54–5
compliments 15, 91
confidence struggles, signs of 87
conversation starters 68–9
courage 8–10, 13, 16, 19–20, 36, 42, 58, 64, 66, 68–70, 74–7, 82, 84
creativity 66, 79

D
dancing 48–9
diets, healthy 43

E
earthing (grounding) 47
effort, praising 91
empathy 90
endorphins 37
environmental issues 76–7

F
failure, attitudes to 86, 87
faking it 19
fear 7–13, 16, 29–30, 32, 34, 38–9, 44–7, 60, 90–2
feelings 11, 16, 51–3, 78, 86–7
fight, flight or freeze 10, 30

foods, trying new 6, 62–3
friends, making 68–9

G
games 61, 69
goal-setting 24–7, 34, 54–6, 79, 84–5, 88
gossip 23
gratitude practice 82–3

H
health 42–3
helping each other 14–15, 16–17, 75

I
imagination 34–5

J
journal writing 78–9

L
laughter 36–7
leading by example 86–7
letter writing 16, 27
listening skills 89
love, unconditional 13

M
meditation 11
meeting people 7, 68–9
mind, healthy 42–3
muscle relaxation 28
music 48–9, 56–7

N
nature, spending time in 46–7
negative thoughts 21, 40–1, 82, 83
nervous system 11, 43
nervousness 8, 9
new things 6, 14, 18–19, 62–3, 70–1, 87, 89
no, saying 9, 22, 72–3, 74–5

P
peer pressure 72–3
physical activity 42, 46, 48–9, 58–9, 70–1
planning skills 60–1, 65, 88
poetry 50–1
positive thoughts 21, 40–1, 83

posture 45, 47
praise 91
present moment, being in the 28–9
problem-solving skills 67, 86
public speaking 7

R
rating confidence 6–7
reflection 78–9, 84–5
relaxation strategies 28, 52, 60
responsibility 21, 93
role play activities 68–9

S
self-care 22, 75
self-esteem 20–1, 42, 59, 85
self-kindness 21, 40–1
self-talk 40–1, 78, 84
senses 11, 29
serotonin 42–3
sleep/sleep diaries 43
solution-focused approaches 88
standing up for yourself 9, 22–3, 72–3
strength 19, 58–9
stress management 31, 36, 43, 52, 59
superheroes 39, 54–5
support 5, 13–17, 33, 36–9, 56, 68–9, 75, 77, 80–1, 88–9
survival skills 64–5

T
talking things through 16–17, 38–9, 87, 90, 92
tension 28, 60
test-taking 60–1

U
uncertainty 12, 86

V
visualization 34–5, 60

W
worry 32–4
writing 16–17, 27, 32–3, 50–1, 78–9